TUDUMM

Gayatri Chowdhary

Feel, fall, rise.

Acknowledgements

This poetry book would not have been possible without the support and encouragement of my Parents and Friends. Special thanks to Dida (my Nani) for being my biggest cheerleader.

Thank you. I feel lucky to have all of you in my life!

Table of Contents

You Are Cute

Milky Way

Maybe fire doesn't like to burn,
its flames burn brighter when it
cries out loud to be calmed.
Maybe ice hates being cold,
and wants to be consumed by heat
and become a part of the air.
And the Earth has always
wanted to touch the sky,
and the rain is the sky's way
of quenching its thirst,
by making water bridge the gap
between the two for a few months.
Maybe the sea keeps moving
and sends out waves because
it wants to call out to the earth.
Maybe you and I, we're not just humans.
Maybe we're stars, living among others
in a galaxy of our own.
Each time we find a star
that makes us shine brighter,
we yearn to form a constellation with it.
What if we're not humans at all?
What if we are stars, beautiful stars,
that perhaps beings from other planets look at,
and call stars?

Birds Like You

How heartwarming it is,
that cute chirpy birds drop by your window
and nuzzle the flowers in your little nurseries.
Maybe they liked something about your home,
or the way you put life and care into your plants.
Maybe the last time they visited you,
your face brightened up,
and they loved your smile,
and they want to see you smile again.
What if they find you as cute as you find them?

Humans are Cats

We humans stretch and yawn,
after a good night's sleep,
and curl up in warm spots,
in moments of freeze.
We love a good snack and gentle cuddles,
from our favourite person,
whom we love to hang out with.

With soft little hairs on the face,
Deep down, we humans are just cats,
A sense of comfort, we always chase.

We love attention, but will pretend not to care,
Don't get too clingy, or we'll give you that bad stare,
We stalk social media, they peek through doors,
Both of us, are always so curious.

We love snuggles and treats,
Deep down, we humans are so feline.
They purr, and we speak with a grin,
There's surely a soul of a cat,
that lies deep within.

Auspicious

So you loved creating art as a kid,
but now you've lost touch,
you're waiting for the perfect moment to draw,
but does it ever come?

Little perfectionist,
when created for self,
art is beautiful, even if it's imperfect.
So embrace the chaos and pick up that pencil -
for you don't have to create the perfect art,
you just have to create something
that makes you feel perfect.

Beautiful

Isn't it beautiful how you are capable
of falling in love with moments?
Moments, so tender and delightful, that they
stay protected deep in your heart braces?
Moments, that you replay on your sad days
and a precious smile spreads instantly across your face!

These movements could have been with anyone;
a kind stranger on your train
who made sure you got out safe,
and didn't miss your stop
because of the overcrowded entrance!
They could be those deep conversations
you had on your first date,
or the fun time you spent with your friends!

It could be that gentle kiss on your forehead,
that felt like a warm hug on a tiring day.
Moments, we fall in love with moments
that pass in a jiffy,
but in our hearts, they stay forever safe.

Hold My Hand, Tight

First Date

If you dig deep into my study closet,
you'll come across a fading train ticket
and maybe a bus ticket as well,
of the day we went on our first date to Mumbai CST,
the memory of it in my mind, is still fresh.
For it rained and I rediscovered an old place with
a new person, who I thought was forever mine.
The place became my favourite
until we parted ways.
And then when I visited it again,
it looked so boring and lifeless,
as though its charm was lost,
maybe it had always been this way!
But our new love was the ambience
I thought this place had set.

We give too much credit to places, you know;
maybe it's the people we go to these places with,
that add all the magic and ambience.

Stone Cold Heart

A lonely heart survives many deaths,
and the stone-cold winter is its most ruthless killer.
The winter morning's chilling air
seeps deep into your heart
and attempts to turn it into a stone.
It's saviour: a warm cuddle
that resurrects the dying heart.
Appreciate the ones that
wake up without cuddles every day.
These lonely warriors
give winters a tough fight.

Tudumm

New people seem so hunky-dory at first,
until you get closer and tap
a world of darkness in them,
that you never knew existed.
It's scary, it's intimidating,
it's anything but flowery.
Like a dark Netflix series,
the more you watch,
the deeper you're pulled
into the character's darkness.
The question is, would you still watch it till the end -
or escape?

Stuck

You like darkness because you've
never
seen
the
light.

Red Pill

Here's a hard-hitting truth.
You can't make him love you,
no matter how much you try.
So gulp it, feel the aching pinch
of your unrequited love,
let it pierce through your heart
and weaken your soul.

Fall.
Stare lifelessly at the wall
as you sit on your sofa,
drenched deep in melancholy.
Gulp down the truth again,
let the teardrops fall,
as you silently zone out
into the oblivion.

•••

• • •

Accept.
Accept that you've been a fool.
That you've got your heart broken, yet again.
Laugh at yourself for being so stupid, yet again.
Laugh at your desperation,
your stupid decisions,
and your bad judgment skills.

Fall.
Imagine you are falling into a cliff,
smile a bit, like you do when you get a sense of relief,
Let the water of stupidity and bad karma
consume you,
one last time.
Fall now, so you cannot fall again.

Delusional

I ask all the butterflies in my heart
to stop fluttering, just to protect myself.
A part of me is happy knowing that somewhere,
in the parallel universe where things are different,
I am yours, and you are mine; all mine.
That picture of us is a thousand light years apart,
and I hope that in another lifetime or
another dimension,
we have made it.

Hits

What cuts deeper than a heartbreak song,
is the moment when you realise
that someone else can relate
to those lyrics,
because of the heartbreak
you caused.

Loop

Is this what life is going to be about? A repeating loop of events? Or do we feel so because of social media? Watching people trying to stay relevant, become relevant, achieve glory, and have it all only to detox their way out of it?

People flirting over Instagram stories, upping their simp game, moving over from the talking stage, to majorly crushing on each other, getting all high on vibes and then closing their chapter. A good time ends, life goes on and on and on and on and on and another song starts trending on Instagram. A music that never took off that well suddenly hits the top 10. Music that you swore you'd never get addicted to becomes an earworm and you find yourself grooving to it as you scroll.

...

●●●

Netflix catches your attention and you watch a nice series that you can finally brag about to your friends who kept debating about it all weekend only to find out that they discovered another cool one. You put up a meme on your IG Story and people respond to it, reactions keep coming in until they stop. And then you're left with a void – that's okay, life goes on and on and on and on and you look up.

You're on the bus, you look around, and everybody around is on their phone. They're all a part of the same loop that you are in. The same loop that you and I will continue being into until; well, until, a song long forgotten becomes a trend and joins into the loop.

We're all in the loop. We're all in the same loop. Is this what life is going to be about? A repeating loop of events? Or do we -

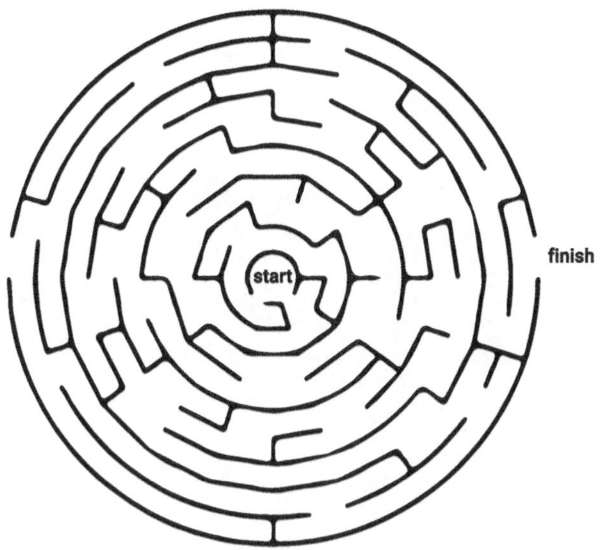

start
finish

Angel

I wish I could tell you everything about meeting you that night. When you drank your beer with a smirk after saying something funny, God, you looked so cute. I wish I could tell you how your dove-like eyes melted my heart. I wish I had ditched my curfew time and spent more time with you that night, just deep-diving into meaningful talks, walking and maybe sneaking into more dessert shops and eating sweet stuff until we got high on sugar. I wish I could tell you how blissful meeting you was; just like a movie. But I'm glad I didn't tell you all about it because it was, after all, a movie, and movies always end, don't they? You watch some and you realise that you don't always get to have the kind of happy ending those movies have. But, watching them helped heal a part of you and become a better version of yourself. I became one because I met you. Thank you :)

Back to December

The guilt of letting you go is eating me alive.
Sometimes I wonder if I'd given us a chance,
perhaps you would have overcome those flaws?
And now you're a better version of yourself,
far less grumpy and kind,
But there's nothing I could do now,
so I resist telling you that
I miss those car rides in your green Skoda,
when we'd hang out as good friends,
and explore different places together
But I guess that's what life is about,
everyone has their *Back to December*,
you'd be that for me, always.

Ctrl + z

So I resist texting you and telling you about my day,
and I calm my heart beats down,
every time I see your texts,
and I don't send you the poems I write about you,
nor the dreamy reels that make me think of you,
because I know that if I do, it won't end well,
so trust me when I ask you to stay away,
I know, you're going to thank me someday.

Last

And when we met for the last time,
I didn't let my hair down or
involuntarily take off my specs,
like I do when I'm with you,
hoping that my messy final look
would make goodbyes easier for you.

Genius

Gifted kids, did you make it?
To the pedestal where they always thought you'd be?
Or did you lose touch with your genius side,
and succumb to the ordinary?
'Scholar', 'ranker', 'genius' they'd always call you,
'She'll achieve something great,'
you were also convinced.
But then you blink your eyes and
see how far others have come -
Big4, USA, Startup Founder,
but you're still here, a lost talent or worse,
Gifted kids - I hope you made it,
and I hope you don't find yourself here,
relating to this piece.

Mask

When they're not looking,
I stop smiling and relax my eye muscles,
take off my mask,
and soak in the pleasure of
a resting bitch face.

Glimpse

Do you ever feel like you have multiple tabs open in your mind? You have stopped opening and reviewing each, and every one of them. Now you open one tab, go through the pictures, read the stuff in bold, and get an idea of the rest of the article. You close it, then move to the other tab. You don't want to get engrossed in a single tab. As you think you'll get too involved in the details, you'll absorb the emotions and sentiment, the pain, and the negatives of the article, so you have kind of trained your mind to detach from it and just *glimpse* through it.

Your glimpses are quick - just the way you ignore the melodrama, the overly cringe moments of songs and movies, and move towards the informative parts. The movie ends and a new web series begins. You meet someone new or old, traverse through another day, and just like that, you *glimpse* through different days in the same way. The weekend ends, and there you are, at the start of a Monday. That's okay, you will *glimpse* through it. And beat the Monday blues.

...

•••

'Same old, same old' you say to an old school friend when they catch up with you through an Instagram story reply. They decide to open up to you, you read their message about a bad time they faced. It's a long message but that's okay, you'll do a quick read, and tackle your mind by switching off your heart at sentences that could potentially be tear-jerking. You have empathy but you have learnt to be strong and detachably empathic, as the last time you decided to go deeper into the glimpse, you ended up shedding a tear.

The last time you experienced physical pain through someone else's horrific pregnancy experience, you almost fainted. The last time you felt emotionally connected to a set of friends, they turned out to be manipulative. The last time you liked a guy, he broke your heart, so you get by life, *glimpse* through it like an article on a tab.

You listen to podcasts on 1.25X to skip the slow, melodramatic pace, you glimpse through life as it keeps you peaceful, but deep down you know how chaotic it would make you feel. But that's okay, maybe you will *glimpse* through your chaos?

Gateway to Dawn

Backspace

A new you was born
the day you realised that,
they aren't worth writing long messages to.

Family

If I could find within my heart,
the faith you have for me,
I would have conquered mountains.
Through every storm.
Your belief in me is my guiding light.
Even in my next birth,
I'd choose to be your daughter again.

Resurrection

But I re-visited Mumbai CST a few years later,
and was surprised to see that
its charm was resurrected again.
It bloomed even more beautifully,
even though solitude was my only company.
Maybe it's also the versions of you
that define a place's beauty.
Your *best* version gets all the magic and ambience.

Forgive and Forget

I know we say 'forgive and forget',
but I've come to realize that when adulting,
'sorry' does not fix things,
it only fixes the ego.
So be mindful of your words,
and don't hurt people just because you think
they'll forgive you easily.
They don't,
They just learn to *forget* the hurt.
So when humanity rewrites the book of idioms,
'forget and forgive' should make it to the pages,
Because fake forgiveness comes instantly,
but true forgiveness only comes with *time*.

Coming Back to Life

One of the best feelings in this world is when you feel the nectar of healing all across your senses. You are happy by yourself and feel the love that you receive from the people who love you. You are no longer forcing emotions, friendships, and relationships. You acknowledge that everything that has happened in your life - whether good or bad, has led you to this peaceful version of yourself. You understand that things and people change for you when you change your perspective towards them. You are free - free from your past, regrets, guilt, and mistakes. Free from that baggage you carried all along. You are free and you feel the beauty within yourself. You feel beautiful inside out. That sounds like a nice feeling, doesn't it? This feeling is not far away. Hang in there, you are almost there. You are almost there.

Dramatic

I wanted to entertain myself,
so I searched for you in a song.
Call me dramatic, but I'll blame it on work from home.
So, I go on Spotify and search for *our* song.
I find it, but I don't feel the aching pinch,
I need something strong.

I look for the one I listened to,
when we met for the last time.
The one that always brought
flowy tears to my eyes.
I listened to it months ago.

Anticipating a punch of emotions,
I open it and play it.
I close my eyes; *well it just adds to the effects.*
I'm halfway through the song,
I swear my mind loves it.
It's a beautiful song indeed,
but where's the sinking feeling?
This is not the pain I signed up for!
So I listen to it once again,
this time while reading the lyrics,
like you'd always recommend.

•••

• • •

A memory flashes through my mind.
That's you on the beach,
you're talking to me,
and I'm listening to you.
You don't look as charming as before.
Okay, focus.
We hold hands.
It seems like a fading memory,
but I can feel the roughness of your palm.
You are staring into my eyes,
but this time, I am only looking at you,
observing you,
judging you.
I'm not tilting my head in overwhelm.

I'm actually distracted by the sea,
the warmth of the air,
the TikToker couple lip-syncing
to a trending song.
If you subtract the melodrama
that followed after, between us,
it was a beautiful-looking day.

• • •

Our song has just ended.
And my smile - it has taken a good shape.
I listen to it once again,
to cherish the beachy vibes.

This melody has a new meaning now.

Senses

Some sensations we carry in our mind pockets,
like the fearful sound of thunder,
smell of the first rain,
taste of polio drops,
the touch of a feather
and a loved one's warm embrace.

Isn't it funny how our mind pockets
don't carry visual memories
in the same way?

We dare to take pride in our sense of sight,
but it is our sense of smell, touch and hearing,
that connect us more deeply to
the essence of *humanity*.

Cover & Illustration Credits

1. **Book Cover** designed by - Khushal Metar
   www.metarkhushal.work

2. **Loop** image generated via - Mazesforfun.com

About the Author

Gayatri Chowdhary is a Mumbai-based creative professional with an enduring love for words and storytelling. With a background in Biotech engineering and Marketing management, her journey into the world of writing began in her college years, when she discovered the power of words to capture and express the intricacies of human emotions. 'Tudumm' is her debut poetry collection, that invites readers to explore a spectrum of emotional themes.

You can check out Gayatri's literary works on Instagram at **@mystiquewrites** and on her website at www.gayatrichowdhary.com

Write to her at author@gayatrichowdhary.com